The Bhagavadgita

The Bhagavadgita is the celebrated epic poem of India. It is, infact, an excerpt from the great Indian epic Mahabharata.

The Bhagavadgita has been translated into every major language of the world—French, Italian, Greek, Spanish, German, Japanese, Russian—and into English by several formidable scholars. Of all the English renderings of the Bhagavadgita P. Lal's version fully preserves the dignity and grace of the original. Shorn of scholarly verbosity and sophisticated interpretations, this is a devoted work of literary beauty with moral and spiritual worth which readers will find deeply moving.

P. Lal teaches English literature at Calcutta University and owns a Calcutta based publishing house workshop, which has given a much needed fillip to Indian writing in English, in original and in translation, which P. Lal prefers to call 'transcreation'. He has transcreated a large number of Sanskrit classics.

"English literature would be incomplete without possessing in popular form a poetic and philosophical work so dear to India."

Sir Edwin Arnold

Rs. 20.00

THE
BHAGAVADGITA

Transcreated by
P. Lal

ORIENT PAPERBACKS
A Division of Vision Books Pvt. Ltd.
New Delhi ● Bombay

ISBN-81-222-0101-6

1st Published   1965
Reprinted   1991

The Bhagavadgita

© P. Lal, 1965

Published by
Orient Paperbacks
(A Division of Vision Books Pvt. Ltd.)
Madarsa Road, Kashmere Gate, Delhi-110 006.

Printed in India at
Gopsons Paper Pvt. Ltd., Noida

Cover Printed at
Ravindra Printing Press, Delhi-110 006.

Transcreator's Note

This edition has been thoroughly revised by the transcreator. Chapter XIV, "The Different Gunas", embodies suggestions made by Professor Gilbert Highet; the first sloka of Chapter I was improved by Professor Alain Danielou; and slokas 13-14 of Chapter XVIII are indebted to a note by Ananda Coomaraswamy in The Journal of the American Oriental Society. Other improvements came from friends too numerous to name individually; I am, however, specially grateful to a review-article by Meena Belliappa in Poetry India which contained many useful suggestions that I have incorporated.

P. LAL

vyamishreneva vakyena buddhim mohayasiva me |
tadekam vada nischitya yena shreyo' ahamapnuyam ||

You bewilder me with confusing speech;
tell me that one truth by which I may find you.

[III : 2]

Introduction

In a short Preface to the first edition of my English version of the *BhagavadGita* (published by Writers Workshop in 1965) I wrote:

"I first transcreated the *Gita* in 1947 in rhymed English verse." (Numerous extracts, including a generous portion of Canto 10, were printed in *The Xaverian,* December 1947). "It was an adolescent experiment and, though a couplet or two may not have sounded too bad, the iambs and anapaests in general appeared to be contrived, precious, and terribly archaic.

"Another attempt in prose, five years later, became too flat. The original has the dignity and memorability of a chanted poem. Prose is too thin a medium for it.

"The essential structure of the *Gita,* however, is question-and-answer. Arjuna questions; Krishna answers. The tone is lofty, but *intimate;* highly serious, but *friendly;* sacred, but *colloquially* so. The present transcreation tries to preserve the dialogue spirit of the Sanskrit, a spirit marked by simplicity, grace, brevity, and clarity. I have tried to retain the *Gita's* sweetness of persuasion and strength of conviction.

"Readers who discover in my version a certain dramatic quality will be right in inferring that I see the sacred text of Hindustan as an integral part of Vyasa's epic of India. In the epic, the *Gita* appears to have only one purpose; to get Arjuna to fight. It is fitted neatly into the grand design of *dharmaksetra Kuruksetra*".

A revised edition appeared in 1968, but I was not entirely satisfied with either version. Arjuna's behaviour on the battlefield—his refusal to fight and kill his relatives—inspired and simultaneously baffled me. It seemed to be out of character. Why should a Ksatriya hesitate to do his military duty? I felt the answer must lie in the *totality* of Arjuna's character, and to discover the totality I embarked on a major project: to transcreate the *Mahabharata* sloka by sloka, hoping in the process to find at least a few clues to clarify at least one of what I consider to be the three focal controversy-points in the *Gita*.

Nine years and one hundred and eleven transcreated fascicules later, I have a few glimmerings, but still not the complete answer (assuming that there is a complete answer). Arjuna is a searching, because troubled, man, unlike his brothers who are satisfied with conventional values. He is the only Pandava brother whose variety of erotic adventures suggests an almost restlessly twentieth century hero seeking self-fulfilment through sexual satisfaction. He marries the princesses of Kalinga, Cedi, Madra, Magadha, and Yavana; in Hardwar he has a son Iravat by Ulupi, the Naga princess; in Manupura, he marries Citrangada and has a son by her named Babhruvahana; in Dvaraka he abducts and marries Krishna's sister Subhadra and has a son by her, Abhimanyu. With the exception of Bhima (who marries the raksasi Hidimba), the other Pandavas are happy with their common wife Draupadi, I suspect that Arjuna's mental make-up is worrying and questing, individualistic, even protestant. He cannot lose (because he possesses the invincible Gandiva bow), yet he will not fight. He prefers to be the world's first pacifist, a conscientiously objecting, bravely quaking and Quaker Hindu. To call him a "coward" as Krishna does (II : 3), is an injustice. It requires a very special kind of courage to be "cowardly" in the Arjuna manner. For Arjuna stands for ahimsa, Krishna recommends killing; Arjuna in the *Gita* is, for whatever reason, the humanist, and Krishna, for whatever reason, is the militarist. And there is no reconciliation between these two fearfully opposed philosophies.

Which leads to the second focal point of debate in the *Gita*—I mean the nature of the Cosmic Revelation in Cantos 10 and 11. A careful reading of the *Gita* will show that Arjuna keeps on questioning and arguing with Krishna until Canto 10. He says

"You bewilder me with confusing speech",   (III : 2).

Quite naturally, for Krishna at one point comes up with a startling suggestion—the atman is eternal; only the body dies; so go ahead and kill—you will kill only the body, the atman will remain unaffected (II : 19-21). There could hardly be a better example of forked-tounge speciousness, and Arjuna is justified in asking if such dynamic "action" is not worse than his passive non-doing based on "knowledge" and conscience.

"If, as you say, Krishna, knowledge excels action,
Why do you urge me to this terrible war?"   (III : I)

The truth of the matter surely is that not rational refutation is possible of the essential humanist position that killing is wrong, especially when such a stand is grounded in a clean conscience and is cleanly argued. Many of the answers given by Krishna appear to be evasive and occasionally sophistic. When logic fails, Krishna apparently resorts to divine magic, to maya. The *Gita* is transformed from a reasoning dialogue in Cantos 1-9 to a poetical and mystical vision in Cantos 10-11. Unable to satisfy a worried warrior's stricken conscience by rational argument, Krishna opts for the unusual—he stuns Arjuna with a glorious "revelation" of psychedelic intensity. He succeeds; from Canto 12 Arjuna accepts whatever Krishna has to offer. Brain is overpowered by bhakti—but is it ethical to silence logic with magic? It seems to me that Krishna employ a confidence trick and, being Divinity, he not only gets away with it but actually is praised in some quarters for providing a climactic darshan. What I mean is that, in the twentieth century, in the contemporary world, apocalyptically threatened by the unchecked proliferation of nuclear mushrooms, Arjuna stands for the voice of invincible conscience; he is the humanist hero who has risen above the demands of military caste and convention-ridden community. His plight on the field of Kuruksetra is not an abstract, condemnable intellectual perplexity that can be juggled away by "Cosmic Multi-Revelation". It is a painful and honest problem that Krishna should have faced on its own terms, painfully and honestly, and did not. Or so the modern critical mind thinks.

The third and last moral and religious insight—there are many others, but these three I consider to be the most stimulating and relevant in our age—comes in Canto 15. Krishna describes a "cosmic fig-tree" whose roots are in the sky, whose fruits are on earth. "Slice this fig-tree with non-attachment," he advises Arjuna, thus ending your karma and obtaining moksa. The co-ordinates of moksa are not given, because freedom, if truly free, can have no limiting co-ordinates, no how-to-achieve-it gimmickry.

The cosmic fig-tree is a metaphor for one of Hinduism's profoundest and subtlest beliefs, a metaphor that has found its way into Indian village folklore as the *kalpa-taru,* the Wish-Fulfilling Tree. The Bengali folksinger Ram Prosad Sen has a song in which he says; "Let's go, my mind, and pluck the four fruits." These are the fruits that hang from the Wish-Fulfilling Tree. Christopher Isherwood retells the parable in his anthology *Vedanta for the West;* I narrated it in my introductory essay "On Understanding India" to Barbara Harrison's *Learning About India* (1977). It is worth repeating, for it helps to make Krishna's point in the *Gita* clear. The story is exquisitely simple.

The proverbial benevolent uncle turns up in a village and finds his nephews and nieces and their friends playing in a hut with toys and make-do twig-and-rag dolls. "Why play with these?" he asks. "Outside is the *kalpa-taru,* the Wish-Fulfilling Tree. Stand under it, and wish. It will give you anything you want."

The children don't believe him. They know the world's not

structured to give you whatever you want. You have to struggle very hard for the smallest reward—and, of course, others always seem to get plums, for they have what is known as "connections."

They smile knowingly. The uncle leaves.

No sooner has he left, however, than they rush to the Tree, and start wishing. They want sweets—and they get stomach ache. They want toys—and they get boredom. Bigger and better toys—bigger and better boredom.

This worries them. Something must be wrong somewhere. Someone is tricking them. What is this unpleasant unsuspected unwanted extra that tags along with the sweets and the toys?

What they have not realised yet is that the Wish-Fulfiling Tree is the enormously generous but totally unsentimental cosmos. It will give you exactly what you want—Krishna says

"this world is your wish-fulfilling cow,"   (III : 10)

and with its built-in opposite. Nothing in this world comes single; everything comes with its built-in opposite. The tragedy of the world is not that we don't get what we want, but that we always get exactly what we want—along with its built-in opposite. Wish it, think it, dream it, do it—you've got it! and, literally, you've had it. That's it—having and being had.

So the children grow up and become, euphemistically, "young adults." They really are just a bunch of over-grown kids, all trapped under the Wishing Tree. Instead of sweets and toys— childish trifles!—they now crave Sex, Fame, Money, and Power, the four sweet fruits that hang from the tree. Bittersweet fruits. There are, truly speaking, no other fruits. There is nothing else to be bad.

They reach out and bite each of these four fruits and get the same bitter after-taste of disappointment and disillusionment. But they go on wishing, because there seems to be little else that one can do under the Wishing Tree. Creatures come and go; the Tree is always there.

Then they grow old, and are stretched out under the tree, lying on their death cots. Pathetic old men and women, kindly referred to as "guru-jana", "respected elders". They lie huddled in three security-seeking groups. The first group whispers, "It's all a hoax. The world's farce." Fools; they have learnt nothing.

The second huddle whispers, "We made the wrong wishes. We'll wish again. This time we'll make the right wish." Bigger fools; they have learnt less than nothing.

The obliging tree quickly grants their last desire. They die—and they get the built-in opposite of the death-wish— they are re-born—and under the same tree, for there is no other place to get born or re-born in.

The parable does not end here. It speaks of lame boy. The young cripple also hobbled to the tree, but was shoved aside by his more agile friends. So he crawled back to the hut and gazed at the marvellous tree from the window, waiting for a chance for him to go and make the wish that lame boys make. What he saw from the window awed and almost unnerved him.

He saw his companions wanting sweets and getting stomach ache, grabbing toys and getting bored. He saw them scrambling for Sex, Fame, Money, and Power, and getting their opposites, and agonising—and not realising the cause of their anguish. He saw them divided into three groups—the Cynics, the self-appointed Wise Guys, and the hope-bereft Death-Wishers. He saw this clearly, with the poignant brilliant sharpness of naked truth.

The spectacle of this cosmic swindle so *impressed* him that he stood stunned in brief, lucid bafflement. A divine comedy, a divine tragicomedy, the panoramic cycle of karma, was being enacted in front of his eyes. A gush of compassion welled in his heart for the victims of karma, and in that gush of compassion the lame boy forgot to wish. He had sliced the cosmic fig-tree with non-attachment.

He stood outside the orbit of the world's ambivalence.

He had, in showing spontaneous compassion, not done the

planned good act, which earns heaven for its doer and leads to better re-birth. The Hindu heaven is a temporary state, because heaven is really a punishment for good deeds.

Nor had he done the bad act, which earns hell, again temporary, after which one is born again. The Hindu tradition feels that no crime is so bad as to deserve an eternity of punishment.

He had not done the absurd act, either, by opting to cop out of the system. After all, my life is my life, and I can take it whenever I want to; there's no one really to stop me.

He had sliced the cosmic fig-tree by doing the "pure act', the act of gratuitous compassion, which gets no reward or punishment, since it lies outside the give-and-take orbit. The pure act— *niskama karma*—is its own reward. Until the gesture of the pure act is made, we are all trapped under the Wish-Fulfilling Tree. The cripple did not *consciously* know this. He stood, in the healing shadow of his compassions and beyond the pale of the Tree, marvelling at the wondrous and complex and dread fabric of the universe, and forgetting to wish. Forgetting—not remembering to forget. He was the "free", the serene man, the genuine candidate for moksa untouched by the world's ambivalence, and by the heaven and hell the world so copiously offers.

The big question is: Is such compassion possible? Krishna says,

> "Act one *must*—the body compels it—true giving-up is renunciation of fruits" (XVIII : II).

Yes, but can the ordinary human being ever give up the fruits of action? Is the carrot dangled by Krishna ever achievable by the plodding, ego-ridden efforts of mankind? Is Hinduism again talking so big and positing goals so idealistic that, with the exception of saints, all must despair of success? Is it reasonable, is it practical to expect Arjuna, trained as a Kastriya, expert in arts of war, to fight without desire to win?

ॐ

1. Arjuna's Indecision

DHRITARASHTRA ASKED :

Tell me, Sanjaya,
what did the Pandavas and the Kauravas do,
gathered on the sacred battlefield of Kurukshetra ?

SANJAYA REPLIED :

Seeing the army of the Pandavas,
Duryodhana went to his acharya Drona, and said :

"Look at this vast army,
under the command of Dhristadyumna;

Heroes all of them, mighty bowmen rivalling **Bhima**
    and Arjuna ;
Yuyudhana, Virata, and Drupada;

Dhristaketu, Chekitana, and the King of Varanasi,
Purujit, Kuntibhoja, and Shaibya;

Yudhamanyu and Uttamaujas,
Abhimanyu, and the sons and grandsons of **Drupada**.

And look at your army too—
I give you the names of our commanders:

First of all, you, Bhishma, Karna, and Kripa;
Ashvatthaman, Vikarna, and the son of Somadatta;

And many others, all well-armed,
eager to die if necessary for my sake.

My army seems weak compared to theirs,
mine marshalled by Bhishma, theirs by Bhima.

Let orders be passed to protect Bhishma ;
let the troops form ranks."

Bhishma, anxious to revive Duryodhana's spirits,
blew fiercely on his conch, like a lion roaring.

Conches, Kettledrums, horns and tabors blew suddenly.
The noise was tremendous.

Standing in their white-horsed chariot,
Krishna and Arujna blew their conches.

Krishna's conch was called Panchajanya,
Arjuna's Devadatta, and Bhima's Paundra.

And Yudhishthira blew his conch of Endless Victory,
Nakula his of Honey Tone,
and Sahadeva his called the Jewel Blossom.

Each blew his own conch—

the supreme archer, the King of Varanasi,
the mighty charioteer Sikhandin,
Dhristadyumna, Virata and the undefeated Satyaki;
Drupada, too, and Darupadi's sons,
and the strong-muscled Abhimanyu.

And thunderous peal after peal,
crashing through heaven and earth,
shattered the morale of Dhritarashtra's camp.

Seeing Dhritarashtra's men eager for war,
and battle impending,
Arjuna lifted his bow and turned to Krishna.

ARJUNA SAID :

Take my chariot, Krishna, between the two camps;
let me know my enemy before I fight him.

Who are the ones gathered here for bloodshed,
flatterers of evil Duryodhana on sacred Kurukshetra?

Krishna took the glittering chariot midfield,
facing Bhisma, Drona and the lords of the earth,
and said:
"Here are the Kauravas, Arjuna."

Arjuna saw, in the camps of both,
his uncles and grandfathers,
his brothers and cousins,
his sons and grandsons,
his friends, teachers, and acquaintances.

He saw his kinsmen assembled for war,
and pity stirred in him.

ARJUNA SAID :
I have seen my kinsmen gathered for war;
my mouth is dry with fear, my limbs refuse to listen
   to me;
trembling seizes me;
my skin chafes, and the divine bow
slips from my hand.

Neither can I stand erect;
my mind whirls
and unholy omens appear before my eyes.

In killing my brothers, Krishna,
I cannot see anything noble—
I do not want this victory, this glory, this happiness.

What is glory to us, Krishna,
What are pleasures and life,
if those who from us deserve glory, pleasure and life,
are ready to fight us, having given up the world's
   delights—
our uncles, sons and our grandfathers,
our teachers, our eldest kinsmen,
our dearest friends too.

I would not kill them,
not for the three worlds, let alone the earth,
   O Krishna.
I had rather they killed me.

18

What joy is there in slaying Dhritarashtra's sons?—
It is a terrible sin.

I will not kill my kinsmen, Krishna;
how could happiness be mine if I murder my
    brothers ?

Their reason obscured by greed,
they may see no evil in the disunion of brothers,
in hate against friends; but we, Krishna,
we, the clear of mind who understand right and
    wrong;
should we not refrain from such evil acts?

Honour disappears in the family
when the family breaks up; and honour disappearing,
impiety takes over.

Where impiety rules,
the women are corrupted; with the women corrupted,
even caste is endangered.

Intermixture of castes spells doom for the family
as well as for the destroyers of the family;
the spirits of the ancestors fall, denied rice-and-water
    homage.

And by this looseness of the destroyers of the family
is the age-old dharma of caste and the family
    destroyed.

We have heard, Krishna,

hell awaits the families which discard dharma.
What a terrible thing it is to kill brothers,
and cast covetous eyes on their land!

Let the sons of Dhritarashtra kill me.
I will not protest.
Better be killed than kill.

SANJAYA SAID

Arjuna flung away his bow and quiver,
and slumped down on the seat of his glittering chariot,
heavy with sorrow.

ॐ

ॐ

2. The Path of Yoga

SANJAYA REPORTED:
Krishna's words to Arjuna, whose mind was heavy
    with grief,
and whose eyes were filled with tears of pity, were :

Your sorrow, Arjuna, is unmanly and disgraceful.
It stands in the way of heavenly fulfilment.

Don't be a coward, Arjuna.
It doesn't become you at all.
Shake off your weakness and rise !

ARJUNA REPLIED :
How can I fight Bhishma and Drona,
fitter objects for my veneration?

Why, it would be preferable to live as a beggar
than kill these great acharyas.
Their murder will stain with blood all my joys and
    feelings
even while I live, even in this world.

Who can say which is better, Krishna,
we defeating them or they defeating us?
Dhritarashtra's *sons* are our enemies.
Killing them would bring us life-long misery.

Paralysed by pity, full of doubts,
I ask for your grace.
I am your worshipper.   Put me on the right path.
Show me what is good for me.

I know of nothing that can remove this sense-killing
    sorrow,
neither tyranny over the gods, nor kingship of the
    earth.

SANJAYA CONTINUED :
These were Arjuna's words to Krishna.
He added, *I will not fight*,
and lapsed into silence.

To Arjuna, sad in the middle of the battlefield,
Krishna, as if smiling, said :

You mourn those, Arjuna,
who do not deserve mourning.
The learned mourn neither the living nor the dead.
(Your words only sound wise.)

Do not think that I did not exist,
that you do not exist,
that all these kings do not exist.

And it is not that we shall cease to exist in the
    future.

To the embodied Atman, childhood, maturity and
old age continue imperceptibly.
And just that happens with the acquisition of a new
    body.
This does not confuse the steady mind.

Heat, cold, pain, pleasure—
these spring from sensual contact, Arjuna.
They begin, and they end.
They exist for the time being.
You must learn to put up with them.

The man whom these cannot distract,
the man who is steady in pain and pleasure,
is the man who achieves serenity.

The untrue never is ;
the True never isn't.
The knowers of truth know this.

And the Self that pervades all things is imperishable.
Nothing corrupts this imperishable Self.

How utterly strange that bodies are said to be
    destroyed
when the immutable, illimitable and indestructible
    Self lives on !
Therefore, rise, Arjuna, and fight !

 Who sees the Self as slayer,

and who sees it as slain, know nothing about the Self.
This, Arjuna, does not slay.
It is not slain.

This is without birth, without death.
It does not become existent after previous
     non-existence;
nor does it cease to exist after previous existence.
This is birthless, changeless, and eternal.
It does not die when the flesh dies.

And if a man thinks of it as imperishable, changeless,
     and birthless.
how can he possibly kill, or make another kill ?

As a person throws away last year's clothes
and puts on a new dress,
the embodied Self throws away this lifetime's body
and enters another that is new.

Weapons do not harm this Self,
fire does not burn it,
water does not wet it,
wind does not dry it.

This cannot be cut, kindled, wetted, dried;
immobile, immovable, immutable, all-pervasive,
this is eternal.

This is unmanifest, unknowable; and unchangeable.
Now you have this wisdom, Arjuna.
now you should not grieve.

Even if it were constantly to be born,
and constantly to die, you should not grieve.

For death is sure of that which is born,
and of that which is dead, birth is certain.
Why do you grieve then over the inevitable ?

All beings are unmanifest in the beginning,
manifest in the middle, and again unmanifest at the end.
Is this a cause for grief ?

Some imagine the Self as extraordinary;
others say it is a miracle,
others have heard it described as a mystery.
Still others have heard of it but remain unconvinced.

I repeat : This embodied Self, Arjuna, is imperishable.
You have no reason to grieve for any creature.

Think of your natural dharma, and do not hesitate, for
there is nothing greater to a warrior than a just war.

Lucky are soldiers who strive in a just war;
for them it is an easy entry into heaven.

But if you persist in being a coward,
your dignity and your dharma are lost;
and you expose yourself to shame.

The world will connect your name with infamy,
and they who once praised you shall think of you as
    a coward.

Your enemies will hurl insults at you.
Arjuna, what could be more demeaning?

Die, and you go to heaven.
Live, and the world is yours.
Arise, Arjuna, and fight!

Equate pain and pleasure, profit and loss,
victory and defeat.
And fight!
There is no blame this way.

The truths of the path of knowledge I have told you.
Listen now to the truths of action.
These two together can break the fetters of karma.

There is no waste of half-done work in this,
no inconsistent results;
an iota of this removes a world of fear.

In this there is only single-minded consistency;
while the efforts of confused people.
are many-branching and full of contradiction.

There is no constancy in the man
who runs after pleasure and power,
whose reason is robbed by the fool's flattery,
who, abiding by the rules of the Vedas,
proclaims that there is nothing else.
The honeyed rituals of the Vedas, promising
    enjoyment and power.
are certain to lead him into fresh births.

The Vedas deal with three qualities.
Know them, detach yourself from them,
keep your poise,
detach yourself from selfishness,
and be firm in your Self.

The Vedas are a useless pond to a person aware of
    his Self,
a pond when water has flooded the land.

Your duty is to work, not to reap the fruits of work.
Do not go for the rewards of what you do
but neither be fond of laziness.

Steady in Yoga, do whatever you must do;
give up attachment, be indifferent to failure and
    success.
This equilibrium is Yoga.

Selfish work is inferior
to the work of a balanced, uncoveting mind; shelter
yourself in this mental stability, Arjuna.
Harassed are the runners after actions' fruits.

With this mental poise,
you will release yourself from evil and good deeds.
Devote yourself to this Yoga—
it is the secret of success in work.

The steadfast in wisdom, the steadfast of mind,
giving up the fruits of action.
achieve the perfect state.

When your mind is no longer obscured by desire,
repose shall come to you concerning what is heard
and what is yet to be heard.

When your mind, so long whirled in conflicting
    thought,
achieves poise, and steadies itself in the Self,
you shall have realised Yoga.

ARJUNA ASKED :
Who is the man of poise, Krishna ?
Who is steady in devotion ?
How does he speak, rest, walk ?

KRISHNA ANSWERED :
He has shed all desire;
he is content in the Self by the Self.

He is steady.   He endures sorrow.
He does not chase pleasure.
Affection, anger and fear do not touch him.

He is not selfish.
He does not rejoice in prosperity.
He is not saddened by want.

He can recall his senses from their objects
as the tortoise pulls in its head.

Objects scatter away from the good but lazy man,
but desire remains.
In the perfect state, however, desire also goes.

Yes, this is true, for the violent senses
rock the reason of the wisest man.

But the steadfast man thinks of me,
and commands his desires.
His mind is stable, because his desires are subdued.

Wanting objects breeds attachment;
from attachment springs covetousness,
and covetousness breeds anger.

Anger leads to confusion,
and confusion kills the power of memory;
with the destruction of memory choice is rendered
    impossible;
and when moral choice fails, man is doomed.

But a person who is established in firmness,
free from pleasure and repugnance,
traversing experience with his senses restrained—
such a person finds tranquillity.

When tranquillity comes, sorrow goes;
a person whose wisdom is tranquil is closest to
    Realisation.

The wavering person possesses no knowledge,
and indeed no incentive to contemplate.
There is no tranquillity for a person who will not
    contemplate;
and there is no bliss without tranquillity.

The mind is the ape of the wayward senses;
they destroy discrimination,
as a storm scatters boats on a lake.

Only that man can be described as steady
whose feelings are detached from their objects.

What is night to all beings
is daylight to the restrained man;
and when dawn comes to all,
night has come for the perceiving sage.

The ocean, deep and silent, absorbs a thousand
     waters.
The saint absorbs a thousand desires,
ending in bliss, which is not for the passionate.

Undistracted, passionless, egoless.
he finds bliss.

Bliss is to be in Brahman, Arjuna,
to suffer no more delusion.
In bliss is eternal unity with Brahman,
though life itself is snuffed out.

ॐ

ॐ

3. The Yoga of Action

ARJUNA ASKED :

If, as you say, Krishna, knowledge excels action,
why do you urge to me this terrible war ?

You bewilder me with confusing speech;
tell me that one truth by which I may find you.

KRISHNA REPLIED :

At the time of a persons's birth, Arjuna,
two methods are offered :
for the contemplative the Yoga of knowledge,
for the active the Yoga of action.

No one reaches the state of rest through inaction;
and abandonment of work does not lead to perfection.
For look, not a moment gives rest, not a moment
     is without work;
the senses, products of Nature, compel all to work.

31

He is a fool and a scoundrel, who, abstaining from
     action,
nevertheless sits and dreams up sensual visions.

But he excels, who commands his senses by his mind,
and continues to exert in the Yoga of work.

Work is superior to inaction;
inaction will not keep even the body together.
Therefore, Arjuna, work, but work selflessly.

All deeds are traps, except ritual deeds.
Hence the need for selfless action.

When the world was created, Prajapati said:
This world shall be your salvation,
this your wish-fulfilling cow.

Worship the gods with this, and they will listen;
and mutually shall the great good come.

The gods shall satisfy your desires.   He is a thief,
who takes satisfaction, and gives back nothing.

They are cleansed of wrong, who eat ritual food;
but the selfish who eat for themselves, eat filth.

Food is the cause of life, from rain is food born;
ritual gives rain,, and ritual is born of Karma.

Karma comes from the Vedas
and the Vedas from Brahma.

His life is futile,
who is not aware of this wheel's revolutions,
who lives merely to wallow in his senses.

But he who is merged in the Atman, content in the
    Atman,
for him deeds are not fetters.

For him there is no significance in action, or inaction—
nor does he need outside help.

Do what must be done, Arjuna, and do it selflessly:
selfless action is the path to Brahman.

Through work did Janaka and others reach
    perfection;
work then for the uplift of your fellow-beings.

Always will people imitate a superior,
following the example set by his action.

I have no duty; nothing not attained and nothing
    to attain,
yet even I persist in work.

For if I were to stop working,
men would follow my example.

If I did not work, the three worlds would crumble,
judgement would blur, chaos follow, and all beings
    perish.

The wise man must act, even as the work-obsessed
    fool does,
but shedding selfishness, and pursuing knowledge.

Leave aside the fool's work-centred reasoning ;
let the learned learn more through selfess work.

By the senses is all action performed;
confused by his ego, man thinks, I *am the doer*.

But the man who sees the nature of Prakriti and
    Karma,
who sees how the senses impose on the senses,
he escapes.

There is no need for the truthknowing to interfere
with the dullwitted workers attached to the senses,
and deceived by the senses.

Offer all your actions to me, and take rest in the
    Atman,
crush hope and the ego, and fight—rid of your
    doubts.

They also escape the fetters of action
who devote themselves to me, in full faith.

But those who carp, and shun my teaching,
and,. confusing themselves, lose clear vision,
they are doomed, Arjuna.

Human beings are guided by nature.

The wisest man must conform to his nature.
How will stubbornness help?

Desire and disgust are the products of nature.
No man should live in the shadow of either—
they are his deadly enemies.

One's own dharma, however imperfect,
is better than another's, however perfect.
Even death in one's own dharma is to be preferred,
because another's dharma can deceive and degrade.

ARJUNA ASKED :

But what is the power, Krishna,
that propels man to wrong-doing against his true
    desire ?

KRISHNA REPLIED :

Greed, Arjuna, and anger,
created by the terrible and heinous rajas-guna.
Treat them as your enemies.

As smoke smothers fire,
as dust films glass,
as womb envelops seed,
so greed destroys judgment.

The implacable flame of greed is the persistent foe
    c f the wise.
It destroys judgment.

The mind, the intellect and the senses are its dwelling
    place;
it destroys the Atman by working through them.

Therefore, Arjuna learn to control the senses from the
    beginning.
Destroy this heinous foe of the Atman.

It is said that the senses are higher than the flesh ;
the mind is higher than the senses;
the intellect is higher than the mind,
and the Atman higher than the intellect.

ॐ

4. The Yoga of Action and Renunciation

KRISHNA CONTINUED :

To Vivasvat I gave this eternal discipline;
Vivasvat told it to Manu, and Manu to Iskhvaku.

So its continuity was assured, and the royal saints
    understood it ;
but as time passed, its significance declined.

Today, because you respect me, and are my friend,
I give you this timeless, mysterious, and profound
    discipline.

ARJUNA ASKED :

But you were born later, Krishna, than Vivasvat;
and yet you say you gave it to him.

KRISHNA REPLIED :

You, and I, have been many births, Arjuna—
I can recall them all, but you cannot.

Though birthless, and unchangeable, and supreme
I am born through my Maya, defying the laws of
    Nature,

When Dharma declines, and wrong-doing flourishes,
I give myself birth, to restore the balance.

And every age witnesses my birth;
I come to protect the good, and destroy the wicked.
I come to re-establish Dharma.

The man who approves the divinity of my birth
and the miracle of my work.
discards his body, and is not born again.

Free from greed, fear and anger,
merged in me, sheltering in me,
purified by the discipline of knowledge,
many have known me.

I satisfy all, whatever the form of worship.
My path is the path all follow, in different ways.

Men worship gods in the hope of material gain—
they know work brings quick results.

Though I am the creator of the four castes on the
    basis of guna and karma,
I am not really their creator, Arjuna.

For I have no eye on the fruits of action,
and work does not fetter me.
That is the right way of looking at things.

Sages in the past, seeking perfection, knew this,
and knowing it, progressed.
Learn from their example, Arjuna.

What is work ? and *What is not work* ?
are questions that perplex the wisest of men.
Let me instruct you on the nature of work.

Karma cannot be explained;
but what is work one must know, and what is not
    work;
and what prohibited work.

who dares to see action in inaction, and inaction in
    action,
he is wise, he is a yogi,
he is the man who knows what is work.

And if he works selflessly,
if his actions are made pure in the fire of knowledge,
he will be called wise by the learned.

He abandons greed ; he is content;
he is self-sufficient;
he works, yet such a man cannot be said to work.

If he forsakes hope, restrains his mind, and
    relinquishes reward—
he works yet he does not work.

He is satisfied with whatever comes,
unaffected by extremes, free from jealousy,

maintains a balance in failure and achievement—
his deeds do not fetter him.

His karma disappears, his work is all ritual;
he is free from greed and is steady in knowledge.

"The ritual is Brahman, the offering is Brahman,
given by Brahman in the fire of Brahman"—
such absorption in Brahman takes him to Brahman.

Some yogis sacrifice to the gods,
others pay homage by offering the Atman in the fire
of Brahman.

Some offer their senses as homage,
others offer the objects of the senses.

Some offer the work of the body and the vital breath
    of life,
in the fire of selfcontrol, lit by knowledge.

Some offer wealth, others penance, and still others
    Yoga ;
some, controlled and dedicated, offer wisdom and
    learning.

Some channelise the vital breath of life ;
still others, digesting food, offer the body's functions.

All these have realized the meaning of ritual dis-
    cipline and are purified by it ;

they eat remnants of such ritual, and reach the
   eternal Brahman.
Even this world is not for the man without ritual,
how will he gain a better one, Arjuna ?

Innumerable rituals are described in the Vedas ;
they are all the products of work.
If you know this, you shall be saved.

The sacrifice of knowledge is superior to material
      sacrifice ;
action should culminate in wisdom.

Humble yourself, serve others ;
ask questions, and you shall know ;
the wise who have reached truth, will instruct you.

Knowledge will remove your bewilderment,
and you shall see all creation in yourself and in me.

The raft of knowledge ferries the worst sinner to safety.

As a flaming fire consumes logs into ashes,
knowledge consumes karma.

There is no purifier like knowledge in this world :
time will make man find himself in himself.

The devoted man, indefatigable commander of his
   senses, gains knowledge ;
with this knowledge he finds the final peace.

The ignorant, the disrespectful, the disbelieving,
  await ruin.
The doubt-ridden find joy neither in this world nor
  in the next.

Work will not fetter him who shelters in the Atman.
Discipline purifies his work, Arjuna,
and knowledge dissipates his disbelief.

Slice with the sword of knowledge this disbelief in the
  Atman !
Disbelief is the product of ignorance.Arjuna!
Find strength in discipline, and rise,

ॐ

5. The Yoga of Renunciation

ARJUNA ASKED :

You recommend renunciation, Krishna, as well as
    activity.
Which is better ?—Tell me clearly.

KRISHNA REPLIED :

Renunciation and activity both liberate,
but to work is better than to renounce.

He is the constant sannyasi, who is neither depressed
    nor elated ;
free from extremes, his salvation progresses.

The ignorant, not the learned, think the two are
    different.
If one is practised in earnest, the rewards of both are
    received.

The strivers in work reach the fulfilment of the strivers
    in renunciation.

43

See both as the same, and you see the truth.

Renunciation is very difficult, Arjuna ;
but the sage, spurred to work by wisdom, soon finds
    Brahman.

A man who commands his senses and vanquishes his
    body,
who sees one's Atman as the Atman in all,
who purifies his mind before he performs his deeds—
such a man is not sullied.

Though seeing, listening, smelling,
eating, walking, sleeping, breathing,
talking, holding, and discarding, he should say,
I do nothing at all,
firm in the truth it is only the senses that rest on their
    objects.

As a lotus leaf will not be stained by slime,
so the detached person, offering his deeds to Brahman,
will not be stained by work.

The yogis work with the body, the mind and the
    senses,
but abandon greed, in order to purify the Atman.

Abandoning the fruits of work, the balanced mind
    attains tranquillity;
but the unsteady mind, motivated by greed,
is trapped in its own reward.

The firm person, renouncing work through knowledge,
neither acts himself, nor forces action on others,
but takes refuge in the body, the city of the nine gates.

Brahman is concerned neither with the doer nor the
    deed,
nor the reward of the deed.

Brahman does not cause anyone's reward or
    punishment.
Wisdom is blocked by ignorance, and delusion is the
    result.

But, like the sun, knowledge reveals Brahman
to those whose ignorance is removed by
self-realization.

Washed in the light of knowledge, and never born
    again, are those
whose minds are engrossed in the Atman, whose
    fulfilment is in the Atman.

A Brahman, a cow, a dog, an elephant,
are all the same to an Atman-knower.

He has transcended life,
he reposes in Brahman,
his mind is not nervous and agitated.

Reposing in Brahman, and maintaining serenity,
undeluded, the knower of Brahman is not happy with
    what is pleasant,

45

nor unhappy with what is unpleasant.

Unaffected by material phenomena, he enjoys the
    bliss of the Atman.
He achieves eternal peace, sunk in the meditation of
    Brahman.

Restlessness is the product of sensual joys,
joys that are impermanent, joys that begin and end.
The wise do not seek pleasure in them.

He is reposed, he is happy,
who has no anger, who has no desire.

Whose contentment lies within, whose repose is
within, whose glory is within,
that yogi finds Brahman, and is liberated.

All evils discarded, all doubts erased, all senses
    restrained,
devoted to service, he is liberated.

There is the peace of Brahman for all who strive
    thus,
their passions controlled, and their Atman realised.

Controlling his vision, curbing his life breaths,
commanding his senses, mind and intellect,
rid of lust, anger and greed, he finds moksha.

For he knows me as the giver of ritual and religious
    discipline,
the creator of the three worlds, and the refuge of all
    beings ;
and he finds peace.

6. The Yoga of Meditation

Whoever does his work selflessly combines renunciation and activity—
not one who does not work, or rejects the prescribed
duties.
Right action is really renunciation.

The man desirous of Yoga seeks action as the path ;
when Yoga is achieved, serenity takes over.

Then he is not bound either to sense-objects or to
work,
then he is rid of all desires.

The Atman is the means of spiritual achievement.
On no account should the Atman be harmed.
It is your best friend, do not make it your worst
enemy.

It is a friend of the man who uses it to subdue it ;
an enemy of the man who does not.

The Atman is a consummation to the tranquil-minded
and the self-subdued,
who are serene in heat and cold, disgust and delight,
honour and infamy.

When a clod of earth, stone, and gold become alike,
serenity is achieved.

Serenity is achieved by a man who considers impar-
tially his friends, his lovers,
his enemies, his judges and his kinsmen, the sinful
and the wicked.

Living in solitude, with the mind's and body's
passions in check,
a yogi should strive for absorption in the Atman.

And he should seat himself on a clean spot, not
too high and not too low,
spread over with a piece of cloth, and a skin, and
Kusha grass,
and, fixing his mind on a single goal, subduing the
demands of the eager senses,
he should struggle in Yoga, to cleanse his heart.

And he must hold his body still, his head and neck erect,
not let his eyes stare, but gaze only at his nose's tip.

Tranquil and courageous, an avowed brahmachari,
his mind subdued, his thought focused on me.
he must sit, considering me his ultimate goal.

Thus absorbed, thus steadfast,
lost in me, he will find bliss, and the bliss beyond
    bliss, called
Nirvana.

Yoga is not for the glutton, or one who fasts too
    much ;
it is not for the sleepheavy or the sleepless.

Yoga destroys despair ;
it is only for the moderate in eating and resting,
in sleeping and working.

You become tranquil
when the subdued mind is established in the Atman,
when anxiety is overcome, and desires abandoned.

The flame of a windless lamp is never fitful—
a good simile for a controlled yogi, absorbed in Yoga.

When the mind is steady in Yoga, and achieves
    tranquillity,
and when the Atman reveals Brahman, when one is
    contented in the Atman ;
when perfect bliss comes, comprehended by the
    liberated Atman
(a goal from which there is no straying),
and when, having achieved this ineffable state, no
    anxiety disturbs—
Yoga is won!
And this is achieved after much hardship.

Forsaking all desire, and controlling all his senses,
the yogi must not think of anything else.
Success will come by slow degrees.

Should his fickle mind stray,
he must subdue it, reclaim it, and guide it by the
    Atman.

The supreme bliss is found only by the tranquil yogi,
 whose passions have been stilled.

His desires washed away,
the yogi easily achieves union with Brahman.

He sees the Atman in all beings, and all beings in
    the Atman,
for his heart is firm in Yoga.

Who sees me in all things, and all things in me,
he is never far from me, and I am never far from him.

He worships me and lives in me, whoever he might be,
for he has achieved unity of being, he sees me in all
    things.

He treats delight and suffering everywhere as his own,
he is the supreme yogi.

ARJUNA SAID :

You have told me this Yoga of peace and unity of
    being,
but my mind is restless, I do not understand what
    you say.

51

For the mind, Krishna, is powerful, fickle, violent
and uncontrollable.
Harnessing the mind, is like harnessing the wind.

KRISHNA REPLIED :

The mind indeed is all that you say, Arjuna,
but determination helps; and renunciation curbs it.

Without determination, no man can reach Yoga,
but the self-disciplined, struggling nobly, can achieve
it.

ARJUNA ASKED :

What happens to the well-meaning man who does not
·succeed in Yoga,
whose mind wanders, who loses control—
does he not plummet down, is he not doomed
like a tattered cloud ?

Remove this doubt, Krishna—
you seem to know everything.

KRISHNA REPLIED :

He need not fear, Arjuna, neither now nor later—
the struggle for virtue is never wasted.

He reaches the worlds of the blessed, and lives there
a long time;
then he is reincarnated in the homes of the prosperous
and the righteous.

Or he finds birth among learned yogis—
a difficult birth to obtain, very difficult.

There he gets back his former intelligence,
and once again struggles in Yoga.

His primary struggle continues its momentum.
Even a man who merely asks to be enlightened in
    Yoga
is superior to the performer of mechanical rituals.

The yogi who perseveres, revolves through numerous
    births
before reaching the supreme goal.

Be a yogi, Arjuna,
for the yogi is above those who do penance,
above the learned, and above the active workers.

And even among yogis, he is the best
who communes with me in his Atman.

ॐ

ॐ

7. The Yoga of Knowledge

KRISHNA CONTINUED :

Listen, Arjuna, to how you can come to me,
by sheltering in me, and practising Yoga.

I will tell you all knowlege, all realisation,
knowing which, there is nothing more to know.

Out of thousands one perhaps strive for perfection,
and one perhaps of those who strive actually finds me.

Earth, water, fire air, ether ; mind, intellect, and
     egoism—
these make up Nature.

This is the lower Nature
but different from this is the higher Nature—
the principle of life which sustains the worlds.

These two, the womb of all life, are in my power ;
I am the birth and dissolution of this universe.

There is nothing superior to me, Arjuna :
the worlds depend on me as pearls hang on a string.

I am the salt of the ocean, the brilliance of the moon
    and the sun:
I am *Om* in the Vedas, and sound in the sky, and
    manliness in man.

I am fragrance in the earth, and brightness in fire:
I am life in all, and penance in the pure ones.

Consider me the undying seed of all life :
I am the glory of the glorious, and the wisdom of
    the wise.

I am the pure and selfless strength of the strong :
I am desire too, desire that does not transgress
    Dharma.

They are all mine, the states of sattva, and rajas, and
    tamas ;
I am not in them : they are in me.

These three manifestations of the three gunas deceive
    the world,
and it fails to recognise me, because I am beyond
    them.

It is difficult indeed to pierce this divine maya of the
    gunas.
But the faithful are able to pierce it.

The ill-minded and the ignorant are victims of maya,
and do not worship me.

There are four types of good men who worship me,
    Arjuna :
the sorrowing, the truth-seeker, the seeker of bliss,
    and the wise man.

The wise man, steadfast, devoted to me, is the best
    among these.
I love the wise man, Arjuna ; he is dear to me.

They are all good, but the wise man is as my own
    self :
his mind is balanced, he is devoted to me as the
    supreme goal.

After many births, the wise man reposes in me,
    convinced that I am all ;
such a pure soul is difficult to come across.

There are other, made blind by various desires,
who adhere to various rites,
prostrate themselves before various gods, according
    to their natures.

I make firm the devotion of any worshipper,
no matter what his form of worship is.

And with that devotion he progresses in worship,
and obtains his desires, which I alone offer.

But the reward for men of small intelligence is small.
The worshippers of the gods go to the gods.
Who loves me comes to me.

I am formless, but the foolish think I have form.
They do not understand my real nature.

I am covered by maya, and all do not see me.
I am birthless and deathless.
This world of illusion does not understand me.

I know what is, what was, and what will be;
but none knows me.

The play of ambivalence, of disgust and delight,
flings all beings into delusion.

But holy men free themselves from extremes,
and become my devoted worshippers.

They strive for salvation from death and old age,
they shelter in me :
they understand Brahman and the nature of Karma.

They continue in knowledge till the time of death,
    for they are firm in reason :
They know the *adhibhuta*, the *adhidaiva*, the
    adhiyajna, and the *adhyatman*.

ॐ

ॐ

8. The Nature of Brahman

ARJUNA ASKED :

What is Brahman, and *adhyatman*, and Karma ?
What is *adhibhuta*, and what is *adhidaiva* ?

And what is *adhiyajna*, and how ?
And how will the self-restrained realize you, at the
    time of death ?

KRISHNA REPLIED :

The Indestructible is the supreme Brahman,
and its existence in separate persons is *adhyatman*
Karma is the momentum that commences the birth
    of beings ;

the destructible is *adhibhuta*, and the male principle
    is *adhidaiva* ;
and I am *adhiyajna* in the human body.

He attains my being, abandoning his body,
whose concentration at the time of death is on me.
Do not doubt this.

58

Whatever his concentration is on,
he achieves that at the time of death.

Therefore, think of me—and fight!
your meditation focused on me, you will achieve me.

Absolutely unwavering,
consistently absorbed in the male principle, the
Purusha, the mind reaches him.

He achieves Purusha who, at the time of death,
is steady and devoted; has fixed his life-breath
through the power of Yoga between his eyebrows,
and who thinks thus :
The Purusha is all-knowing, lord of all, the ancient,
smaller than an atom, incomprehensible of form,
    dazzling as the sun,
and free of the veiling darkness of maya.

I will now tell you
of what the learned in the Vedas conceive as the
    Imperishable,
which is achieved through the self-control of
    brahmacharya.

He achieves the supreme goal, who forsakes his body
with his senses all restrained, absorbed in yogic
    meditation.
and on his lips the syllable *Om*, symbol of Brahman.

The yogi who every day keeps me in his mind, cons-
    tant and steadfast,

finds me easy of attainment.

He reaches the supreme perfection, and he achieves
    me ;
for such a pure soul there is no more the sorrow of
    rebirth.

Even the world of Brahma cannot escape rebirth ;
but there is no rebirth once I am achieved.

The man who understands day and night
can also understand the thousand-yuga day of
    Brahman,
and his thousand-yuga night.

When the day of Brahma commences,
all forms evolve from the unmanifested ;
when night commences,
they dissolve into the unmanifested.

And this swarm of beings, successively reborn,
dissolves as the night of Brahma commences,
and emerges with the commencement of another day.

But beyond this unmanifested,
there is another Unmanifested, the undyin reality,
which does not dissolve though all beings dgissolve.

This Indestructible and Unmanifested is the supreme
    goal : this is Brahman ;
this is the state of perfection, from which there is no
    rebirth.

Only complete worship of him in whom all things
    repose,
of him who pervades all the worlds,
can obtain this supreme perfection.

I will tell you of time which makes yogis return to
    the world,
and not return.

Fire, brilliance, daytime, the bright fortnight, and the
    six-month course of the northern sun—
this takes the knowers of Brahman to Brahman.

Smoke, night time, the dark fortnight, and the six-
    month course of the southern sun—
this takes the yogi to the lunar brilliance,
but he returns.

Rightly are they thought absolute, these bright and
    dark paths :
for one results in non-return ; the other causes return.

The yogi who understands the nature of these paths
    is not deceived ;
therefore, Arjuna, make yourself firm in Yoga.

For the yogi is above the rewards offered in the
    Vedas, above ritual, penance and charity—
he alone understands the nature of Reality, he alone
    finds the supreme goal.

ॐ

9. The Secret of Work

I will give you the profoundest of secrets, Arjuna,
leading to perfection,
for you are not cynical.

This is the most perfect of sciences,
of secrets the most profound, and of salvations the
supreme ;
this you will understand immediately, and perform
without difficulty.

Disrespectful men, ignoring this, fail to attain me,
and fall into fearful rebirths.

My invisible presence straddles this universe :
all beings have life in me but I am not in them.

Look at my miraculous Yoga, Arjuna—
even beings are not in me!
Though it creates and sustains beings,
my Self is not established in them.

62

As the tremendous wind reposes in the sky
though it seems to travel everywhere,
so all beings repose in me.

And when a day of Brahman ends, all beings return
    to my Nature ;
when a day begins, they emerge again.

I vitalise my Prakriti, and this swarm of beings is
    evolved,
all subordinate to Prakriti.

But those acts do not affect me, Arjuna—
I am neutral, unattached.

Under my supervision, Nature turns out the animate
    and the inanimate ;
this is the reason the world forever keeps spinning.

The ignorant fail to recognise me in my human form,
because they are not aware of my status as lord of
    all beings.

Hollow of hopes, hollow of deeds, hollow of
    knowledge,
they are like rakshasas, swamped by delusions.

But the mahatmas have knowledge of my
    transcendent nature :
they consider me the changeless source of beings,
they adore me with singleminded devotion.

They worship me, and sing my praises ;
they strive resolutely for me ;
they pay homage to me, and are always constant.

Others worship me as the all-formed, as unity, as
    manyformed, as separate :
each worships as best as he can.

I am the ritual, the sacred gift, and the sacred tree,
I am the holy food, the mantra,
I am the sacred fire and the sacred offering.

I am the father and mother of this world,
I maintain it and purify it ;
I am the goal of knowledge,
I am *Om*, and the three Vedas;

The supporter, the refuge, the lord, the silent witness,
    the friend,
the origin, the dissolution, the storehouse, and the
    seed.

I offer heat : I send and withhold rain :
I am death and moksha, Arjuna :
I am what is, I am what is not.

The learned in the three Vedas worship me and drink
    the *soma* juice,
and purified, they pray for heaven ;
reaching the world of Indra, they enjoy the pleasures
    of the gods.

Having enjoyed heaven, they return to the material
    world
because their virtues have been sufficiently rewarded.
Those who adhere to the worlds of the Vedas, are
    doomed to constant rebirth.

But those who worship me and my unity in all beings
    are the truly preserving,
and to these I give what they have not and increase
    what they have.

Even the worshippers of idols, in reality worship me;
their faith is real, though their means is poor.

For I am the lord and enjoyer of all ritual :
but because they do not know me, they are born
    again.

The worshippers of the gods achieve the gods ;
of the fathers, the fathers ;
the worshippers of the spirits go to the spirits
who worships me, comes to me.

I will accept any gift,
a fruit, a flower, a leaf, even water,
if it is offered purely, and devoutly, with love.

Whatever you do, Arjuna, whatever you sacrifice,
whatever you give in charity, whatever penance you
    perform.

do it for my sake.

This will free you from the fetters of work,
and you will come to me, with your heart steady in
   Yoga.

All beings are the same to me, Arjuna :
I hate none, I love none ;
but those who are my devoted worshippers,
they are in me, and I am in them.

If the most wicked of men acknowledges me as
   supreme above all,
regard him virtuous, Arjuna : he has chosen the true
   path.

Soon will he become purehearted, and achieve undying peace.
I promise you this : no worshipper of mine is ever
   rejected.

Sheltering in me, all will achieve the supreme
   goal—
women, Vaishyas, Shudras, and all of low birth.

Small wonder then that pious Brahmins and steadfast
   saints find me!
Give up this brief joyless world, Arjuna and strive
   for me.

Immerse yourself in thoughts of me, be my
    worshipper,
offer sacrifice to me, and prostrate yourself before
    me.
I tell you this, Arjuna : with your heart steadfast,
and your mind concentrated on me alone,
you will certainly come to me.

ॐ

10. The Universal Glory

KRISHNA CONTINUED :

Listen to my Supreme wisdom, Arjuna :
I speak for your good, because you are dear to me.

Neither the gods nor the saints have understood my
　　divine origin ;
for I am the cause of the birth of the gods and the
　　saints.

Whoever knows me as birthless, without beginning,
　　and the supreme master of universe,
he of all mortals sees clear, and is absolved of taint.

Intellect, knowledge, vision, perseverance, truth and
　　renunciation.
gentleness, joy, sorrow, birth, death, awe, fearlessness,
ahimsa, equanimity, penance and charity, fame, and
　　sense of shame—
these human states arise from my being alone.

The seven saints and the four founders of the human
    race were products of my mind ;
from them was born this swarm of life.

This is the truth.
The man who knows the difference between illusion
    and reality is the yogi.

I am the source of everything, everything evolves
    from me—
thinking in this manner, the learned concentrate on
    me.

Their minds immersed in me,
their senses in me,
instructing each other and singing my glory,
they are happy.

And I enlighten them, and they come to me, for
they are devoted and steadfast

I dwell in their heart,
and my compassion like a glowing lamp of wisdom
dispels the ignorant darkness in them.

ARJUNA SAID :

Your are the Supreme Brahman, the supreme goal,
    the supreme purifier ;
Narada, Astia, Devala, and Vyasa have called you
    eternal,
selfglowing Purusha, the first god ;

and this is now your own revelation.

All that you say to me is true, Krishna ;
neither the gods nor the demons comprehend your
    essence.
You alone know yourself by yourself, transcendent
Purusha ;
you are the source of life, the lord of life,
the god of gods, the lord of the world.

Speak to me of your divine powers which sustain the
    world and are your existence.

How shall I achieve you, Krishna ?
What should be the objects of my meditation ?

Narrate your Yoga and your glory at length,
such nectar from your lips is what I desire.

KRISHNA REPLIED :

I shall narrate you my divine glories in ordered form
there is no end otherwise to them.

I am the Atman, conscious in the heart of all life ;
and I am also the beginning, the middle, and the
    end of all life.

I am the Vishnu of the Adityas, the glorious sun
among heavenly bodies ;
Marichi among the winds, and the moon among
    planets.

70

Of the Vedas I am Samaveda, Vasava among gods ;
of the faculties I am intelligence; and I am the
consciousness of the world's creatures.

I am Shankara among the Rudras, and Vittesha
among the yakshas and rakshasas ;
I am Pavaka among the Vasus, and among mountains
I am Meru.

Among priests, Arjuna, I am Brihaspati,
Among commanders Skanda, and the ocean among
expanses of water.

I am Brighu among saints, *Om* among words ;
among sacrifices I am Japayajna, and the Himalaya
among steadfast objects.

Among trees I am the fig-tree, and Narada among
holy men,
among gandharvas I am Chitraratha, and Kapila
among saints.

Among horses I am Uchchaishravas, sprung from
nectar ;
among elephants Airavata, and among human
beings king.

Among weapons I am the thunderbolt, and among
cattle the heavenly cow ;
I am sexual desire too, creator of life ; and among
snakes I am Vasuki.

71

Ananta among serpents, Varuna among creature
of the sea ;
the Aryama of spirits of fathers, and the god of death
among governors ;

Prahlada among Daityas, time among measures,
lion among beasts, Garuda among birds ;

Among cleansers I am the wind, Rama among the
courageous ;
the crocodile among fish, the Ganga among rivers.

I am the beginning, the middle, and the end of all
that is flux ;
among wisdoms I am knowledge of the Atman, and
I am truth among disputes.

Among letters I am A, among compounds the
Dvandva ;
and I am immeasurable time, and the many-formed
sustainer.

I am merciless death, and the wealth of the wealthy ;
among female virtues I am fame, beauty, memory,
wisdom, chastity and sweet speech.

Among hymns I am Brihatsama, among metres the
Gayatri ;
among months Margashirsha, and among seasons
spring full of flowers.

I am the deceit of the deceitful, and the strength of
    the strong ;
I am struggle, I am realization, and the virtue of the
    virtuous.

I am Krishna among the Yadavas, and Arjuna
    among the Pandavas ;
among poets I am Vyasa, among ascetics Ushana.

Among punishers I am the mace ; I am the tact of the
    tactful,
the silence of the secretive, and the wisdom of the wise.

I am the germ of life ;
nothing animate or inanimate has existence without
    me.

There is no limit to my divine glory,
you hear but a fragment of my unfathomable
    prowess.

If there is any man powerful, blessed and talented,
his glory is derived from a part of my glory.

But what use to you is this parade of my powers ?—
Have faith in me : know that I exist, and that I
    sustain the world.

ॐ

ॐ

11. The Cosmic Revelation

ARJUNA SAID :

You have destroyed my doubts with your
    compassionate   words,
full of wisdom about the nature of Brahman.

I have heard of your greatness,
I have heard of the birth and death of creatures.

And there is truth in your words, Krishna.
I ask you, Purushottama, give me revelation !

If you think me worthy, Krishna,
I beg of you, Yogeshvara, give me revelation !

KRISHNA SAID :

Look, Arjuna, at my divine forms,
various-coloured, various-shaped, in a bewildering
    panorama.

See the Adityas, and the Vasus, the Rudras, the
    Ashvins and the Maruts ;
see also glories you have never witnessed before.

See the entire universe revolving in me, the animate
    and the inanimate—
see whatever else you wish to see.

I will grant you super-sensuous sight to witness my
    glory—
your mortal eyes are unable to behold it.

SANJAYA REPORTED :

Then Krishna revealed his supreme form—
possessing numerous mouths and eyes, glittering with
    divine ornaments, displaying divine signs,
divinely garlanded, divinely scented, all-shaped, all-
powerful , transcendent and limitless.

Were a thousand suns to explode suddenly in the sky,
their brilliance would approximate the glory of the
    sight.

And in the body of Krishna,
Arjuna saw the separate universes united, and resting.

Struck with awe, his hair on end,
he bent his head, and joined his palms.

ARJUNA SAID :

I see all the gods in your body, O Visheshvara, all
variety of life ;

I see Brahman on the lotus, the saints, and the *nagas*.
I see your form stretching on every side,
arms, stomachs, mouths and eyes, without beginning,
     middle, or end.

I see your crown, your chakra, your mace,
your gathered radiance covering the three worlds.

You are the supreme reality, the end of knowledge ;
the shelter of the three worlds, the protector of
     Dharma, the ancient Purusha.

I see you without start or growth or end, many-
     armed, omnipotent.
The sun and the moon are your eyes, the flame in
     your mouth burns the three worlds.

You fill the interworld space and all things else ;
I shake with fear, the three worlds shake, witnessing
     your awesome form.

These countless gods merge into you, singing your
     praise with palms joined ;
Prosper ! is the chant of the saints and the yogis.

The Rudras, the Adityas, the Vasus, the Ashvins, the
     Maruts,
the gandharvas, the yakshas, the asuras and the
     siddhas—
all marvel, all are spellbound.

76

Seeing your limitless form, many-mouthed, many-
    eyed, many-armed, many-thighed, -bellied, and
    -footed,
the worlds are spellbound, and I am spellbound.

I see you reach the sky, glorious with colour,
with mouths agape, and wide red eyes, and my heart
    knows fear,
my steadfastness disappears ;
O Krishna, peace deserts me.

Take pity, O God, lord of the three worlds.
Seeing your mouths, vivid and with teeth glowing
like fires on the day of dissolution,
my head whirls,
O Krishna, peace has deserted me.

Bhishma, Drona, and Karna, Dhritarashtra's sons,
    kings and warriors,
sweep into your mouth,
between your teeth their heads protrude, dreadfully
    crushed.
Like many small streams rushing to the ocean,
these heroes rush into your flaming mouths.

Like moths rushing to the fatal flame,
these heroes rush into your flaming mouths.

And you chew the worlds in your flaming mouths,
    and lick your lips ;
O Krishna, your shafts of flame brighten the universe.

Tell me who you are, O fiery-formed ;
O Krishna, have pity.
How can I know you ?

KRISHNA REPLIED :

I am time, the supreme destroyer of the three worlds,
here visible in the three worlds.
Even if you refuse to fight, none of these soldiers
    will live.

Wake up, Arjuna, and win glory !
Destroy your enemies and enjoy their kingdom !
Their death is ordained—
you are only the immediate cause.

All have already been killed by me—
Drona and Bhishma, Jayadratha, Karna and the
    others.
Fight ! the day is yours.

SANJAYA REPORTED :

Hearing this, Arjuna, shaking,
prostrated himself before Krishna.

ARJUNA SAID :

It is in the fitness of things, Krishna,
that the world rejoices and sings your praise,
the rakshasas flee in fear,
and bands of devotees stand in silent supplication.

Why shouldn't they ?

Why shouldn't they worship the creator of Brahma,
    the lord of Brahma,
the infinite, the god of gods, the refuge of the three
    worlds ?
You are deathless, you are real, you are unreal, you
    are what is beyond these.

You are the first god, and the primal Purusha ;
the refuge of the three worlds, the knower and the
    known,
the ultimate end.
O Infinite Form, the universe is rich with you !

You are the god of wind, fire, water, and death, you
    are Prajapati ;
I worship you a thousand times, and a thousand
    times again !

May homage flow to you from all quarters !
Your boundless power sweeps the universe,
you are all.

And I have presumed, from love and casual regard,
called you Krishna, Yadava, and friend,
thinking you a friend, unmindful of your glory.
I have lowered you in laughter, in resting, eating and
    walking, alone and in company.
Forgive me, Krishna.

For you are the world's father, the end of its
    supplication, the most mighty.

The three worlds do not know your equal—who can
   surpass you ?

I bend my body to your glory,
and I beg forgiveness of you, my lord !
Be merciful to me,
as a friend to a friend, a lover to his beloved, a
   father to his son.

Though terror shudders in my' heart,
my joy brims over.
O refuge of the worlds, O god of gods, I beg your
   grace,
reveal to me your form !

Let me see you with crown, mace, and chakra.
I long to see you ;
O thousand-armed, show me your four-armed form !

KRISHNA SAID :

My love shows you this supreme revelation, Arjuna ;
none has seen this before.

Neither study of the Vedas, sacrifices, gifts, cere-
   monies, rituals, nor the strictest penance
will reveal me in this form to any other.

Forget your fear and bewilderment.
Throw off your terror, be glad of heart—
and look !

80

SANJAYA REPORTED :

Krishna graced Arjuna with a vision of his peaceful
    form ;
Krishna gave Arjuna peace.

ARJUNA SAID :

Seeing your peaceful form, Krishna,
my peace returns, I am normal again

KRISHNA SAID :

It is very difficult to see what you have seen ;
even the gods hunger for such a vision.

Neither the Vedas, nor penance, charity, nor sacrifice,
can make men see me as you have seen me.

Single-minded devotion alone
can make this form of mine appear.

He reaches me who struggles for me, who has me as
    an ideal,
who is free from desire and is unaffected by anger.

ॐ

ॐ

12. The Way of Devotion

ARJUNA ASKED :

Who are the better yogis, Krishna,
those who steadfastly worship you,
or those who worship the invisible and ineffable
    Brahman ?

KRISHNA REPLIED :

Those who worship me single-mindedly and those
    who have unshakable faith,
are for me the most learned in Yoga.

But those who worship the deathless Brahman,
the imperishable, the unnameable, the invisible,
the immutable, unshakable, and eternal—
they also finally find me.

But their problems are greater :
for finite beings to attain the infinite is difficult.

Those who worship me, offer their deeds to me,
    consider me the supreme goal,

think of me with singleminded devotion—
I am their salvation from the whirlpool of the world.

Put all your mind in me, all your intelligence in me :
and you will certainly live in me for all time.

If you are unable to do so,
at least learn the importance of virtuous habit.

If the art of good habit is difficult,
learn to do everything for my sake—
even that suffices.

If even that is difficult, take shelter in me,
do not hanker after the rewards of your actions.
Discipline yourself.

Knowledge is superior to good habit, contemplation
  is superior to knowledge,
giving up the rewards of actions is superior to
  contemplation.

Dear to me is the man who hates no one, who feels
  for all creatures,
who has shed thoughts of "I" and "mine", who is
  not excited by sorrow or joy,
who is patient and serene, steadfast and subdued.

Dear to me is the man who neither annoys nor gets
  annoyed,
who is free from excitement, jealousy, fear and worry.

Dear to me is the man who is self-sufficient,
chaste, indifferent, determined and decisive.

Dear to me is the man who is neither self-pitying nor
   passionate,
who forsakes deeds, renounces purity and impurity,
   and is devoted.

Dear to me is the man alike to friend and foe,
alike in fame and infamy, in heat and cold, in joy
   and sorrow ;
unattached, equal-minded in blame or praise,
silent, satisfied, undisturbed, singleminded in devotion.

Dear to me are those who walk along this deathless
   dharma,
faithful and devoted, considering me the supreme goal.

ॐ

॥ॐ॥

13. The Field and the Knower of the Field

ARJUNA ASKED :

What is Prakriti and Purusha, the Field and the
    Knower of the Field,
what is knowledge and what is knowable ?

KRISHNA REPLIED :

This body is called the Field,
the man who masters it is called the Knower of the
    Field.

I am the Knower of all Fields ;
what is knowable is knowledge of the Field and its
    Knower.

Listen to me well if you wish to know what the Field is,
    What its qualities are,
what effects are born of what causes,
and also who the Knower is and what his attributes
    are.

Variously have sages sung it, in delightful songs,
in slokas of clarity and power, written to the glory
of Brahman.

The qualities of the Field are these :
the elements, egoism, the intellect and the invisible
mind, the ten senses ;
lust, anger, pleasure and pain ; intelligence, patience ;
and the sum of all these.

Knowledge of the Field consists of the following :
lowliness, non-pride, ahimsa, dignity, tranquillity,
and homage, chastity, selfcontrol, and
steadfastness ;
abandonment of sensual desires, together with absence
of egoism ;
meditation on the defects of birth, age and death,
of sickness and sorrow ;
nonattachment even to son, wife, and home,
singleminded faith in me,
pilgrimage to places of quiet, discontent with crowds ;
persistence in spiritual struggle, awareness of the
end of knowledge.
The opposite of all this is ignorance.

I will tell you what must be known ; knowing which,
immortality is possible.
What must be known is neither being nor nonbeing.

Its hands and feet are everywhere, its ears everywhere;
it stands, straddling the three worlds.

It is radiant with the senses, yet not sensual,
it is despotic, yet it invigorates everything.

It is outside and inside life, it is the animate and the
     inanimate ;
it is ineffable in its essence, it is far and near.

It is one, yet split up into a myriad beings :
it is the sustainer of beings, their destroyer and
     creator.

It is the light of lights, shining through darkness :
it is the only knowledge worth knowing ;
it is the end of knowledge, it exists in everyone's heart.

This is the nature of the Field.
This is the knowledge that must be known.

Prakriti and Purusha are without any beginning,
and all the interplay of the senses is the result of
     Prakriti.

Prakriti is the cause of the body's and the senses'
     evolution,
Purusha the cause of the feelings of pleasure and pain.

Hidden in Prakriti, Purusha experiences the Prakriti-
     produced senses ;
his birth in pure or impure wombs is the result of
     this attachment.

The supreme Purusha is also the Witness, the
    Permitter, the Sustainer and the Enjoyer,
the highest God, the Supreme Soul.

The man who understands Purusha and Prakriti
    exhausts his succession of births.

Some through devotion see the Atman ;
others chose the path of knowledge,
still others follow the path of action.

Still others, unaware of all this, worship by hearsay ;
these also are saved, because they have faith.

Whatever creature is born, animate or inanimate,
is born of the union between the Field and the Knower.

His vision is clear who sees Brahman as equal in all
    beings,
as the non-material in the material.

And seeing Brahman equal in all beings,
he takes care not to injure Brahman by the Atman,
and achieves the supreme goal.

His vision is clear, too,
who sees all actions as the work of Prakriti,
and the Atman as unaffected.

And when he sees behind the scattered existences
    of all beings an essential unity,
he becomes Brahman.

Beginningless and feelingless, this unchangeable
    Atman
neither acts nor is affected by acts, though it is
    lodged in the body.

As the all-embracing sky is pure though it spreads
    everywhere,
so the Atman, everywhere scattered, remains always
    pure.

As a single sun illuminates this vast earth,
so he who lives in the Field illuminates the entire
    Field.

And those who can distinguish clearly between the
    Field and the Knower
eventually reach the supreme goal.

ॐ

14. The Different Gunas

KRISHNA SAID :

I will now give you the greatest knowledge of all,
through which the sages have achieved perfection.

They are not subject to rebirth at the time of creation,
nor are they affected at the time of the world's
 dissolution.

The great Prakriti is my womb, and I place the seed
 in it ;
in this way, Arjuna, life begins.

Remember : whatever form of birth there is in this
 world,
the great Prakriti is the ultimate womb, and I am
 the seed-giving father.

Sattva, rajas and tamas—
these Prakriti-produced gunas unite the body to the
 Atman.

Sattva unites with its purity and luminosity ;
its points of reference are happiness and knowledge.

Rajas is the quality of passion, and causes unrest
    and attachment :
it unites by creating attachment to action.

Tamas is born of ignorance ;
it unites throug hunknowing, torpor and sleep.

Sattva refers to happiness, rajas to action ; .
tamas, stifling discrimination, to unknowing.

Sattva occasionally rules over rajas and tamas ;
rajas over sattva and tamas, and tamas over sattva
    and rajas.

When the light of wisdom penetrates every sense,
sattva is predominant.

Cupidity and desire to work, restlessness and passion,
are born when rajas rules.

Darkness, sloth, misunderstanding and delusion,
are born when tamas rules.

And if the Atman meets death during sattva's pre-
    dominance,
it straightaway reaches the pure regions of the
    knowers of wisdom.

Death in rajas means birth among the action-
   obsessed ;
death in tamas means birth among the unreasoning.

The fruits of noble action are sattva and gentle ;
the fruits of rajas agony, of tamas ignorance.

Wisdom is the result of sattva and lust of rajas ;
ignorance, misunderstanding and delusion of
   tamas.

The sattvika go up, the rajasika hang in midspace,
the tamasika, caught in the lowest guna, go down.

When the sage sees no other worker but the gunas
and sees also what is beyond the gunas,
he reaches me.

The Atman which transcends these matter-involved
   gunas
is untouched by birth and death, decay and sorrow,
and finds immortality.

ARJUNA ASKED :

How is one to know one who has transcended the
   gunas ?
how does he behave, what does he do with his life ?

KRISHNA REPLIED :

He does not dislike light, he does not dislike work,

he does not desire them when he is without them ,
he behaves detachedly ;
he knows the gunas are working, and he remains
    steady ;
he remains serene in pain and joy, or when
    considering a piece of earth, a stone or a lump
    of gold,
he remains serene in moments of glory and shame ;
he remains serene in honour and dishonour,
he has abandoned all worldly undertakings.
Such a man is said to have transcended the gunas.

My unflinching devotee
transcends the gunas and is ready for union with
    Brahman.

For I am the abode of Brahman, the deathless and
    the unchanging,
the abode of eternal Dharma and supreme felicity.

ॐ

ॐ

15. The Highest Purusha

KRISHNA CONTINUED :

Mention is made of a cosmic fig-tree rooted above,
whose leaves are supposed to be the Vedas ;
the knower of this fig-tree is the knower of the Vedas.

Its branches reach out below and above,
and the gunas nourish them ; its flowers are the
objects of the senses ;
below the ground flourish more roots, giving birth to
action.

You may not see its real shape, nor its end, birth
and existence ;
slicing this fig-tree with nonattachment, a man
should desire the end of karma,
sayirg : I shelter in the Purusha that caused the birth
of the eternal cycle.

Free from vanity, delusion, and attachment,
passions under control, and unmoved by opposites,

The anti-divine confuse what should be done with
  what should not be done :
they have neither virtue, nor good conduct, nor truth.

They say :
The world is false and immoral, godless, and born of
  lust.

With these beliefs, these poor people
become the world's enemies and its potential
  destroyers.

Hypocritical, vain and fierce, inflated with
  over-reaching ambition,
they let their ignorance breed evil thoughts, and
  strive for the world's ruin.

Tormented by endless worries which only death ends,
considering sensual pleasure as the only end in this
  world,
locked in their lust, ambition, and anger, they run
  after sensual delights.

"Today I enjoyed this, tomorrow I'll enjoy that ;
this I have, that I'll get tomorrow ;
I killed this enemy today, tomorrow I'll get rid of
  the others.
I am king ; I enjoy, I know success, power and
  pleasure.
I have untold wealth, I was born auspicious.
What man is like me ?"

the clear-thinking man finds the supreme goal.

The sun does not illumine it, nor the moon, nor fire;
this goal is my abode, and to achieve it means the
  end of karma.

An eternal fragment of myself becomes an Atman in
  the wordly cycle,
and pulls the Prakriti-bound mind and senses to
  itself.

So Brahman enters a body or discards it,
like a breeze picking up the fragrance of flowers.

Supervising the ear, the eye, touch, taste and smell,
and also the mind, he enjoys the objects of the senses.

The unintelligent do not see him transmigrating,
or living in the gunas or even enjoying them,
but the wise do.

Struggling yogis see him in themselves,
but the less subtle and wise, in spite of their devotion,
fail to do so.

The light living in the sun which illumines the world,
the light in the moon and in fire, are mine.

Nourishing the earth with energy, I sustain life ;
becoming the fluid moon, I feed plants.

And living in life as the vital breath,
I chew the four kinds of food.

I live in all hearts ;
memory and feeling, lack of memory and lack of
    feeling proceed from me ;
I am what the Vedas want to know,
I am knowledge of the Vedas, and the knower of
    the Vedas.

Two kinds of Purushas exist in the world, the
    perishable and the imperishable :
bodies are the perishable, the self is the imperishable.

Another, the Supreme Purusha, is the Highest Soul,
the deathless Lord, whose energy sustains the three
    worlds.

I am above the perishable and the imperishable ;
therefore the world and Vedas call me the Highest
    Purusha.
The man who sees me as the Highest Purusha
is the man who adores me with his whole heart.

I give you this profound teaching
in the hope that you will reach supreme wisdom.

ॐ

16. Divine and Demonic Natures

KRISHNA CONTINUED:

The divinely-born have the following qualiti
absence of fear, a clean heart, firmness in th
    knowledge,
charity, persistence, sacrifice and study of s
simplicity, integrity, nonviolence, truth, n
    modesty, kindness, and absence of evil
courage, compassion, and selflessness.

Pride, obstreperousness, vanity, anger, boo
    ignorance
are the marks of the anti-divine.

Divine birth leads to moksha, and a
    bondage.
Do not fear, Arjuna, your birth is divi

Two kinds of people inhabit this ea
    and the anti-divine ;
the divine I have explained to you ;
the anti-divine.

Deluding themselves, whirled in their own
    bewilderment,
slaves of the ego, they fall into a horrible hell.

Vain, selfish, and obsessed with possessions,
they pay lip service to virtue ;
insolent and passionate, they loathe the Atman
in themselves and in others.

I cast these foolish sinners
always in the wombs of anti-gods.

Born from anti-divine wombs, and ignorant from
    their birth, they fail to reach me,
and become even worse in their next birth.

Hell has three gates—lust, anger, and greed ;
for your own sake, Arjuna, give up these three.

If a man gives up these three evils, and is absorbed
    in his own improvement,
he may find the supreme goal.

But the man who ignores the rules of the scriptures,
and is moved to action by impulse and lust,
never finds perfection ;
no happiness for him, no supreme goal.

The scriptures should tell you what should be done
    and what avoided :
your actions should conform to the truths of the
    shastras.

ॐ

॥ॐ॥

17. The Three Devotions

ARJUNA ASKED :

What is the condition of those who set aside the
    scriptures
but perform their duties with devotion ?
Is it sattvika, rajasika, or tamasika ?

KRISHNA REPLIED :

Let me tell you what it is.
The Atman knows three types of devotion.

Each person's nature dictates his manner of
    devotion :
a man is what his faith is.

For which reason, sattvika men worship the gods,
the rajasika worship the rakshasas, the tamasika
    spirits and ghosts.

And anti-gods are worshipped by men
who torture the Atman with lust and selfishness,

100

and reject the disciplines laid down in the scriptures.

Food, discipline, charity—all are different with
    different people.
Let me explain this to you.

The sattvika likes food to be pleasing,
healthful, oily, and substantial.

The rajasika likes food to be bitter, sour, dry,
    burning ;
food that produces pain, sorrow, and disease.

The tamasika likes leftover food cooked three hours
    earlier,
stale, malodorous, and tasteless.

Work which is sattvika is work performed selflessly,
for its own sake, not for reward.

Work which is rajasika
is work for reward, performed for the sake of fame
    and success.

Work which is tamasika
is work without any kind of dedication,
work that goes against moral principles.

Discipline of the body means worshipping gods and
    Brahmins ;
it involves wisdom and purity, brahmacharya and
    ahimsa.

Discipline of speech means speaking the truth ;
it involves pleasant and helpful words, and study of
the Vedas.

Discipline of the mind means serenity ;
it involves silence, self-control, compassion and
honesty.

These are the three aspects of sattvika.
They are practised by men who have devotion.

Discipline used for reward, honour or fame,
is rajasika—it is transient and treacherous.

Discipline practised for self-torture, from **folly or**
malevolence,
is tamasika.

Sattvika charity is
giving for the sake of giving,
giving that expects no taking,
giving at the right time to the right person.

Rajasika charity is reluctant giving,
giving that expects return,
giving that looks for recompense.

Tamasika charity is
giving to wrong people at the wrong time,
giving without concern, giving **with** pride.

Brahman is *Om Tat Sat*, the Truth that is :
Brahmins, Vedas and rituals proceed from the Truth
    that is.

Chant *Om*,
when you give charity,
when you practise discipline,
when you perform ritual.

Chant *Tat*, which is Brahman.
And *Sat*, which is Truth and Goodness.

Firmness in discipline and charity is *Sat*.
Any action thus performed is *Sat* ; it is real.

Unreal is action with discipline,
charity without sympathy,
ritual without devotion.

ॐ

ॐ

18. The Way of Salvation

ARJUNA SAID :

Tell me, Krishna,
the truth about renunciation, about salvation
   through it.

KRISHNA REPLIED :

Renunciation means the giving-up of desire-laden
   action ;
it also means abandonment of action's fruits.

Some thinkers say all work should be renounced ;
others prefer not to renounce rituals, charity, and
   discipline.

But let me tell you the truth—
renunciation is of three types.

Rituals, charity and discipline should not be
   renounced.
They purify their performer.
But their fruits must always be renounced—

104

that is final.
Duties should not be renounced.
Only the tamasika types renounce duties.

Nor should threats of fear and pain be reasons for
 · renouncing
(as the rajasika argue).

Duties performed without attachment or hope of
reward are known as sattvika work.
The true renouncer, whose doubts have been dispelled,
neither likes pleasant duty nor dislikes an unpleasant
    one.

Act one *must*—
it is only the fruits that are renounced.

Action brings either pleasant, unpleasant, or mixed
    fruits after death.
The true renouncer escapes them, the reward-seeker
    does not.

Learn from me the wisdom of Samkhya.
All work is ruled by five causes—
matter, agent, motive, motion, providence.
Material, formal, efficient and divine causes
govern body, speech, and mind.
That is why the man who thinks the Atman alone is
    the agent

is a fool—he knows nothing.

But the selfless man of clear vision,
though he kills, does not really kill—
for he is not tainted by his action.

Knowledge, the Known, and the Knower are the
    causes of action.
The instrument, the object, and the agent are the
    bases of action.

Knowledge, action, and agent are of three kinds,
    says Samkhya.
Let me explain them to you.

Knowledge that sees Brahman everywhere, the one in
    the many,
is sattvika.

Knowledge which sees difference everywhere,
everywhere variety,
is rajasika.

And that which sees only lies, pettiness and disunity,
is tamasika.

Action performed without love or hate, without desire
    for its fruit,
is sattvika.

Action performed with desire, pride, and struggle,
is rajasika.

106

Action performed blindly, foolishly, and ruinously,
is tamasika.

An agent free from attachment, unaffected by success
    or failure,
is sattvika.

An agent who is passionate, ambitious, and
    temperamental,
is rajasika.

An agent unsteady, boorish, arrogant, dishonest,
    malicious, lazy, and despondent,
is tamasika.

The mind is of three types too ; so is discipline—
let me explain.

The mind that knows the difference between work
    and renunciation,
right and wrong, bondage and liberation, fear and
    fearlessness,
is sattvika.

The mind that is muddled on the meaning of dharma
is rajasika.
The dark mind that thinks vice is virtue
is tamasika.

The discipline that organises the mind, the

life-breath, and the senses,
is sattvika.

The discipline that leads to wealth, success, and
 honour,
is rajasika.

And that which breeds sloth, fear, grief, worry, and
 conceit,
is tamasika.

There are three types of joys.
The joy which is first poison but in the end nectar,
the joy enjoyed almost as a habit by the transparent
 mind,
is sattvika.
The joy of sense pleasures, first nectar, then poison,
is rajasika.

The joy of self-delusion, bred by sloth and folly.
is tamasika.

There is nothing on earth, nothing in heaven,
that is not the product of the three gunas.

Then there are the four castes, with their different
 duties—
the Brahmins, Kshatriyas, Vaishyas and Shudras.

Duties for the Brahmin :

control of the mind and senses, patience, honesty, knowledge,
and belief in an after-life.

Duties for Kshatriya :
courage, bravery, cleverness, fearlessness, generosity,
and knowing how to rule a kingdom.

Duties for the Vaishya:
tilling the land, cattle-rearing, and trade.
For the Shudra : service.

Each following his conscientious duty, each finds perfection.
Let me explain how this happens.

Perfection is achieved when Brahman is worshipped
to the best of one's ability.

One's own dharma, however imperfect, is a safer guide
than the dharma of another, however perfect.
Conscience is what matters.

Follow your duty, Arjuna, as your nature dictates it.
All work fetters, as all fire gives smoke.
Only selfless duty saves.
Detachment, discipline, desirelessness, renunciation—
these bring true freedom.
Let me tell you briefly how Brahman is reached,
Brahman, the end of all knowledge.

When the mind is pure and the intellect subdued,
when love and hate no longer affect a person ;
a lonely spot is sought, little is eaten,
meditation is practised, the ego surrendered ;
"I" and "mine" disappear, peace is attained.
These are the preconditions of achieving Brahman.

Once Brahman is achieved,
there is no more sorrow, no more desire,
there is only serenity.

Then does the yogi really know my nature,
what and who I am.
He knows me, and becomes me.

And though he work, my grace makes him free.
He works under the auspices of my grace.

Fix your mind on me, Arjuna.
Surrender all deeds to me.

All problems will be solved by my grace.
Pride can only lead to your moral ruin.

If, filled with pride, you say, *I will not fight*,
it is all in vain, you are foolish.
Fight you will, your nature will make you fight.

Your karma will make you fight.
You are foolish.   You will fight in spite of yourself.